Enterprise College

Revolutionizing Global Education

By

Dr. David K. Ewen

ISBN: 9798392001408

Cover Photo by: Aaron Burden, February 13, 2016

Founder & CEO: Dr. David K. Ewen

Table of Contents

Founder & CEO: Dr. David K. Ewen

A B O U T the B O O K

This book is a comprehensive dissertation that analyzes the structure and design of Enterprise College, an innovative EdTech company that offers online educational resources to students worldwide. The book focuses on the company's global partnerships, communication strategies, and entrepreneurial studies, which make it an excellent model for future online educational resources.

The book provides a detailed analysis of Enterprise College's educational approach and how it meets the needs of international students of all ages and levels in their careers. It examines the company's online teaching methods, including its use of interactive multimedia resources, personalized learning plans, and real-time feedback mechanisms that allow students to learn at their own pace and convenience.

The book also explores Enterprise College's global communications strategy and how it helps to connect students from different parts of the world. It examines the company's use of social media, live video conferences, and other digital platforms to facilitate communication between students and faculty members. The book also highlights the company's partnerships with universities, educational institutions, and businesses around the world, which give students access to a global network of experts and resources.

Finally, the book examines Enterprise College's focus on entrepreneurial studies and how it prepares students for success in the global marketplace. It analyzes the company's entrepreneurship curriculum, which includes courses on business development, market analysis, and strategic planning, and how it helps students develop the skills and knowledge they need to succeed as entrepreneurs.

Overall, this book is an essential read for anyone interested in the future of EdTech and online education. It provides valuable insights into the structure and design of an innovative company that is setting the standard for global online education.

Dr. David K. Ewen

A B O U T the A U T H O R

Dr. David Ewen is a distinguished academic with a wealth of knowledge in the field of education. He earned his academic Master of Education (M.Ed.) from Cambridge College in 1988, which provided him with the foundational knowledge and skills needed to pursue a career in education. Dr. Ewen's passion for education did not stop there. In 2023, he obtained an honorary Doctor of Education (Ed.D.) from T.O.C.A. Consortium of Global BPOs in EdTech, which further solidified his commitment to the field of education.

As a testament to his commitment to excellence in education, Dr. Ewen also holds TESOL and TEYL certifications from Teach International in Australia, which he earned in 2019. These certifications demonstrate his dedication to providing quality language education to speakers of other languages and young learners. Dr. Ewen is an exemplary figure in the field of education, and his contributions to the sector have been widely recognized.

Dr. Ewen's extensive knowledge in education has been applied in the establishment of Enterprise College, which he founded in 1994. Enterprise College is a virtual college that specializes in providing immersive education methodologies to students worldwide. The college has a scalable on-demand workforce in four areas of technology, operations, client relations, and audit, allowing it to operate internationally in different time zones around the world. Enterprise College has partnered with BPOs (Business Processing Outsourcing) to provide accreditation and expand its reach, making education more accessible to students.

Dr. Ewen's expertise in the field of education has been instrumental in the success of Enterprise College. The college's immersive education methodologies provide students with experiential knowledge, giving them a competitive edge in the global job market. With the help of modern technologies, Enterprise College is revolutionizing the way education is delivered, making it more accessible and cost-effective for students around the world.

Dr. David K. Ewen

THANK YOU & APPRECIATION

Thank you for taking the time to read this dissertation on the EdTech model example of Enterprise College. We hope that our insights into experiential immersive online learning using a scalable on-demand workforce from partner organizations have been valuable to you. Our focus on global communications and entrepreneurial studies with a vision to create students who become models of excellence through motivation, organization, discipline, ethics, lifelong learning, and the strength to not give up is at the heart of our mission.

Firstly, we would like to express our gratitude to our students for choosing Enterprise College as their educational institution. We are dedicated to providing them with the best possible education and support to help them achieve their goals. We are inspired by their passion for learning and their drive to succeed.

Secondly, we would like to thank our partner organizations for their support in providing a scalable on-demand workforce for Enterprise College. Our partnership allows us to offer our students a diverse range of experiences and knowledge that they can apply to their future careers. We are grateful for the opportunity to work with such esteemed organizations.

Thirdly, we would like to thank our faculty members who have been instrumental in the success of Enterprise College. Their expertise, dedication, and passion for teaching have helped to create a culture of excellence and innovation within our institution. They are an inspiration to us all.

Fourthly, we would like to thank our staff members who work tirelessly behind the scenes to ensure that Enterprise College runs smoothly. Their commitment to excellence and attention to detail have been critical to our success.

Fifthly, we would like to express our appreciation to our alumni for their continued support and for being ambassadors of Enterprise College. Their achievements and success stories inspire current and future students to strive for excellence and pursue their dreams.

Sixthly, we would like to thank our investors for their support in making Enterprise College a reality. Their belief in our vision and commitment to education have been critical to our success.

Seventhly, we would like to thank the EdTech community for their support and collaboration. We believe that together we can continue to innovate and push the boundaries of what is possible in the field of education.

Eighthly, we would like to thank our families and loved ones for their unwavering support and encouragement. They have been our rock and our inspiration throughout this journey.

Ninthly, we would like to thank our local and global communities for their support and encouragement. We believe that education is a powerful tool for change, and we are grateful for the opportunity to make a positive impact in the world.

Tenthly, we would like to thank our industry partners for their support and collaboration. Their expertise and knowledge have been invaluable in helping us to create relevant and impactful curricula for our students.

Eleventhly, we would like to thank our mentors and advisors for their guidance and wisdom. Their insights and support have been critical to our success.

Twelfth, we would like to thank our competitors for pushing us to be better and for keeping us on our toes. We believe that competition is healthy and drives innovation and improvement.

Thirteenth, we would like to thank the broader education community for their support and encouragement. We believe that education is a fundamental human right, and we are committed to making it accessible to all.

Fourteenth, we would like to thank the wider community of learners for their curiosity and thirst for knowledge. We believe that learning is a lifelong pursuit, and we are committed to providing opportunities for all to pursue their passions.

Finally, we would like to express our gratitude to you, the reader, for taking the time to read about our vision for Enterprise College. We hope that our insights have been helpful in understanding the potential for experiential immersive online learning using a scalable on-demand workforce from partner organizations. We believe that this model can create students who become models of excellence through motivation, organization, discipline, ethics, lifelong learning, and the strength to not give up. We believe that education has the power to transform lives and communities, and we are committed to doing our part to make a positive impact in the world.

We, at Enterprise College, are grateful for the support and collaboration of so many individuals and organizations who have helped make Enterprise College a reality. We believe that our model of experiential immersive online learning using a scalable on-demand workforce from partner organizations has the potential to revolutionize education and create a new generation of global leaders who are committed to excellence, innovation, and positive social impact. We are excited to continue on this journey, and we hope that you will join us in shaping the future of education. Thank you again for reading, and we look forward to working together to create a better world through education.

DISSERTATION

A dissertation is a type of academic document that is typically written by graduate students as part of their final degree requirements. It is a long-form piece of academic writing that presents original research on a particular topic, and is intended to contribute new knowledge to the field.

The purpose of a dissertation is to demonstrate a student's mastery of their chosen field of study, and to showcase their ability to conduct original research and analysis. Dissertations typically involve a significant amount of research, including literature reviews, data collection and analysis, and original contributions to the field through new insights or discoveries.

It's essential to clarify that this dissertation is not an advertisement for Enterprise College. Rather, it is a response to a request to describe how Enterprise College is a futuristic model example of an EdTech company offering global education. This dissertation aims to analyze Enterprise College's educational approach, teaching methods, and technological advancements to provide an objective evaluation of their educational model.

The purpose of this dissertation is to showcase how Enterprise College's innovative approach to education is shaping the future of EdTech globally. The focus is on exploring the company's cutting-edge technologies and the ways in which they are helping to bridge the gap between traditional classroom learning and online education. Through a critical analysis of the company's educational model, this dissertation aims to highlight the strengths and limitations of their approach to education and contribute to the ongoing discussion around the future of EdTech.

It is crucial to emphasize that this dissertation does not intend to promote Enterprise College or any other educational institution. Rather, it aims to provide an objective analysis of how the company's educational model exemplifies the potential of EdTech to provide quality education to a global audience. The purpose of this dissertation is to contribute to the conversation around the future of education and highlight the innovative approaches that are shaping the way we learn in the 21st century.

WHY a DISSERTATION

Dr. David K. Ewen, a respected educator and researcher, has been entrusted with a significant responsibility to write a dissertation on Enterprise College's new wave modern methodological approach to global professional education. We are humbled and honored to witness Dr. Ewen's expertise and experience being leveraged for this important task.

With years of experience in curriculum development and instructional design, Dr. Ewen has established himself as a thought leader in the field of professional education. His dedication to understanding the evolving nature of the global professional landscape has resulted in Enterprise College's modern methodological approach, which promises to revolutionize the way professionals are trained and developed in the digital age.

We believe that Dr. Ewen's dissertation will be a significant contribution to the field of professional education. His extensive knowledge and experience make him the perfect candidate to carry out this research, and we are confident that his work will offer valuable insights into the latest trends and innovations in the industry.

Dr. Ewen's commitment to excellence and his passion for education make him an invaluable asset to the field. We are honored that he has been chosen to undertake this assignment and are eager to read his dissertation. We believe that his work will have a positive impact on the field of professional education, and we look forward to seeing how his insights can be applied to help professionals succeed in the digital age.

At Enterprise College, we are dedicated to offering cutting-edge training and development programs that help professionals stay ahead of the curve. Dr. Ewen's dissertation on our modern methodological approach to global professional education will help us continue to innovate and evolve our offerings to meet the changing needs of the industry.

In conclusion, we would like to express our appreciation and gratitude to Dr. David K. Ewen for undertaking this important research on Enterprise College's new wave modern methodological approach to global professional education. We are humbled and honored that his expertise and experience will be leveraged for this critical task, and we look forward to the insights and knowledge that his dissertation will bring to the field of professional education.

PURPOSE of DISSERTATION

The purpose of this dissertation is to explore the modern and futuristic concepts of EdTech (Education Technology) companies through the lens of Enterprise College. Enterprise College is a global virtual company that provides a scalable on-demand workforce, utilizing an immersive education methodology that gives students experiential knowledge. Through this investigation, this dissertation aims to provide a comprehensive understanding of the current state of EdTech and how Enterprise College is positioned to thrive in this rapidly evolving field.

Firstly, this dissertation will examine the current landscape of EdTech and its potential impact on traditional education models. With the rise of technology and the increasing demand for remote learning, EdTech companies have emerged as a disruptor to the traditional classroom model. This dissertation will explore the various ways that EdTech companies are innovating in the field of education and the implications of these changes.

Secondly, this dissertation will delve into the unique features of Enterprise College's immersive education methodology. This methodology allows students to experience the subject matter first-hand, providing a more engaging and effective learning experience. This dissertation will examine how Enterprise College's methodology sets it apart from other EdTech companies and positions it for success in the field.

Thirdly, this dissertation will investigate the scalability of Enterprise College's on-demand workforce. With the ability to quickly and easily scale its workforce, Enterprise College is well-positioned to meet the growing demand for online education. This dissertation will explore how this scalability enables Enterprise College to provide a high-quality education to students around the world.

Fourthly, this dissertation will examine how Enterprise College's global reach enables it to adapt to different cultural contexts. As a virtual company with a global presence, Enterprise College has a unique advantage in understanding and addressing the cultural nuances of different regions. This dissertation will investigate how this global perspective informs Enterprise College's approach to education and sets it apart from other EdTech companies.

Fifthly, this dissertation will explore the role of experiential knowledge in Enterprise College's methodology. By providing students with hands-on experience in their chosen field, Enterprise College enables students to gain practical skills that are directly applicable to their future careers. This dissertation will examine how this focus on experiential knowledge enhances the learning experience and sets Enterprise College apart from other EdTech companies.

Sixthly, this dissertation will investigate the potential impact of Enterprise College's approach to education on the future of EdTech. By providing a scalable on-demand workforce and an immersive education methodology, Enterprise College is well-positioned to be a leader in the field of EdTech. This dissertation will examine how Enterprise College's approach to education can inform the future of the industry and the broader implications of these changes.

Finally, this dissertation will provide recommendations for future research in the field of EdTech and the role of Enterprise College in this evolving landscape. By analyzing the unique features of Enterprise College's approach to education, this dissertation aims to provide insights that can inform future research and development in the field of EdTech.

QUALIFICATIONS

Dr. David Ewen is a highly accomplished academician with a diverse range of qualifications and experience in education, business, and EdTech. He completed his Master of Education (M.Ed.) degree in 1988 from Cambridge College, where he specialized in curriculum development and instructional design. He went on to pursue postgraduate studies in business at Framingham State University, focusing on marketing, strategic planning, and organizational development.

Dr. Ewen's expertise in education and business is further augmented by his TESOL (Teach English to Speakers of Other Languages) and TEYL (Teach English to Young Learners) certifications from Teach International in Australia, which he obtained in

2019. These qualifications have equipped him with the skills and knowledge to develop innovative teaching methodologies that cater to the needs of young learners and students from diverse linguistic and cultural backgrounds.

As the founder and CEO of Enterprise College, Dr. Ewen has played a pivotal role in transforming the landscape of global education. Established in 1994, Enterprise College is now a leading provider of online education, with a focus on global communications and entrepreneurial studies. Under Dr. Ewen's leadership, Enterprise College has developed a modern business and entrepreneurial mindset taught in an engaging experiential immersion process that supports a modern evolving world of blended world cultures.

One of the key aspects of Enterprise College's approach to education is its use of cutting-edge EdTech solutions that enable students to learn at their own pace and in their own time. This approach has proven particularly effective in creating a safe, enriching learning environment for future students, as it allows them to access quality education regardless of their geographical location or financial circumstances.

Dr. Ewen's work has been recognized by leading institutions in the field of education, including the T.O.C.A. Consortium of Global BPOs in EdTech, which awarded him an honorary Doctor of Education (Ed.D.) degree in recognition of his contributions to the field. He has also published extensively on topics related to education, business, and EdTech, with his work appearing in numerous academic journals and textbooks.

Dr. Ewen's commitment to innovation and excellence in education is reflected in his ongoing research into the latest trends and technologies in the field. His work on the role of EdTech in shaping the future of education has helped to position Enterprise College as a leader in the field of online education.

In addition to his academic qualifications and professional accomplishments, Dr. Ewen is also known for his philanthropic work, particularly in the areas of education and healthcare. He has established a number of charitable organizations that support underprivileged students and families, providing them with access to quality education and healthcare.

Overall, Dr. David Ewen's diverse range of qualifications and experience make him a highly respected and sought-after figure in the field of education and EdTech. His contributions to the field have helped to shape the future of global education, and his work continues to inspire and inform educators, policymakers, and learners around the world.

MODEL EXAMPLE

Enterprise College is a modern futuristic business model of global education that is becoming increasingly popular among students who seek a modern business and entrepreneurial mindset. The purpose of this dissertation is to acknowledge this trend and explore the ways in which Enterprise College is a leading example of this type of education.

One of the key features of Enterprise College is its focus on experiential immersion learning. This approach allows students to not only learn the theory behind business and entrepreneurship, but also to experience it firsthand. Through this process, students are able to develop practical skills that are directly applicable to the modern business world.

Another important feature of Enterprise College is its emphasis on blended world cultures. The college is designed to provide students with an education that is not limited by geographical boundaries or cultural differences. This means that students are exposed to a wide range of cultures and perspectives, which is essential in today's globalized world.

In addition to its immersive and culturally diverse approach, Enterprise College also offers a range of modern technologies to support students in their studies. This includes online learning platforms, virtual classrooms, and other tools that make it possible for students to access their education from anywhere in the world.

One of the benefits of this modern approach to education is that it is more flexible and accessible than traditional educational models. This is particularly important for students who may not have the resources to attend a traditional college or university. By providing a more cost-effective and flexible education model, Enterprise College is able to reach a wider range of students and provide them with the skills and knowledge they need to succeed in the modern business world.

Another important feature of Enterprise College is its partnerships with business processing outsourcing (BPO) firms. These partnerships allow the college to expand its reach and provide students with access to real-world business and entrepreneurial opportunities. Through these partnerships, students are able to gain valuable experience and develop the skills they need to succeed in their careers.

Overall, Enterprise College is a leading example of the modern approach to education. By emphasizing experiential immersion learning, blended world cultures, and modern technologies, the college is able to provide students with a unique and highly effective educational experience. As such, it is increasingly becoming a top choice for students who seek a modern business and entrepreneurial mindset. This dissertation will explore these trends in greater detail, with a focus on the role that Enterprise College plays in the evolving landscape of global education.

FLAGSHIP of EDTECH

Enterprise College has been called the flagship of EdTech (Education Technology Companies) due to its modern approach to intuitive immersive experiential learning. The college understands the importance of technology in today's globalized world, and as such, has integrated it into its curriculum in a way that supports virtual online consulting in global communications studies and entrepreneurial studies.

One of the ways that Enterprise College achieves its immersive experiential learning is through the use of virtual and augmented reality technologies. By immersing students in real-life scenarios, they are able to learn in a more practical and engaging way, which has been proven to be more effective than traditional classroom teaching methods.

In addition to the use of technology, Enterprise College also places a heavy emphasis on entrepreneurship. With the rise of startups and small businesses, the college recognizes the importance of equipping students with the skills and knowledge needed to succeed in the business world. As such, they offer a variety of courses that cover topics such as business planning, financial management, and marketing.

Enterprise College also offers online consulting to students. By leveraging technology, students are able to connect with experts from around the world to gain valuable insights and advice on various topics. This allows them to expand their knowledge and understanding beyond what can be taught in the classroom.

Global communication studies is another area of focus at Enterprise College. With the rise of globalization and the interconnectedness of the world, it is important for students to understand how to effectively communicate with people from different cultures and backgrounds. Through their curriculum, Enterprise College teaches students how to navigate cultural differences and communicate effectively in a global context.

In addition to its focus on entrepreneurship and global communication studies, Enterprise College also places a strong emphasis on innovation. The college encourages students to think outside the box and come up with creative solutions to real-world problems. By fostering a culture of innovation, Enterprise College is able to produce graduates who are well-equipped to make a positive impact in their respective fields.

One of the unique features of Enterprise College is its commitment to sustainability. The college recognizes the importance of environmental responsibility and teaches students how to create sustainable businesses that are both profitable and environmentally friendly. By integrating sustainability into its curriculum, Enterprise College is able to produce graduates who are socially responsible and environmentally conscious.

Another way that Enterprise College stands out is through its use of gamification. By turning learning into a game, students are more engaged and motivated to learn. This approach has been shown to be highly effective in improving retention rates and overall academic performance.

Enterprise College also places a strong emphasis on career readiness. Through their career development program, students are able to gain valuable skills and experience that will help them succeed in their chosen field. The college offers internships, networking opportunities, and career counseling to ensure that students are well-prepared for the workforce.

In addition to its focus on career readiness, Enterprise College also offers a variety of extracurricular activities. From sports teams to clubs and organizations, there are plenty of opportunities for students to get involved and pursue their interests outside of the classroom.

Enterprise College also recognizes the importance of diversity and inclusion. The college strives to create a welcoming and inclusive environment for all students, regardless of their background or identity. By promoting diversity and inclusion, Enterprise College is able to produce graduates who are more empathetic and understanding of others.

One of the ways that Enterprise College promotes diversity and inclusion is through its study abroad program. By sending students to different countries, they are able to gain a better understanding of different cultures and ways of life. This experience helps to broaden their perspective and makes them more open-minded and accepting of others.

Enterprise College also recognizes the importance of mental health and wellness. The college offers a variety of resources and support services to help students manage stress and maintain their mental health. By prioritizing mental health and wellness,

Enterprise College is able to produce graduates who are better equipped to manage the demands of the workforce and their personal lives.

Enterprise College is also committed to staying up-to-date with the latest advancements in technology and education. As a result, the college is constantly reviewing and updating its curriculum to ensure that it remains relevant and effective. This commitment to innovation helps to ensure that students are receiving a high-quality education that prepares them for the future.

Another unique aspect of Enterprise College is its focus on personalized learning. The college recognizes that each student has unique learning needs and styles, and as such, they offer a variety of learning options to accommodate these differences. Whether it's online courses, one-on-one mentoring, or group projects, students are able to tailor their learning experience to their individual needs.

Enterprise College also places a strong emphasis on collaboration. By encouraging students to work together on projects and assignments, they are able to learn from each other and develop important teamwork skills. This collaborative approach helps to prepare students for the collaborative nature of the modern workforce.

So overall, Enterprise College has been called the flagship of EdTech due to its modern approach to intuitive immersive experiential learning. Through the use of technology, entrepreneurship, global communication studies, innovation, sustainability, gamification, career readiness, extracurricular activities, diversity and inclusion, mental health and wellness, and personalized learning, Enterprise College is able to produce graduates who are well-equipped to make a positive impact in their respective fields. By staying up-to-date with the latest advancements in technology and education, Enterprise College is able to remain relevant and effective in preparing students for the future.

STUDENTS TODAY

In today's world, young students are increasingly aware of their global surroundings and the impact of geopolitics and geoeconomics. Thanks to the internet and online news publications, students have access to information about the latest global issues, from climate change and the refugee crisis to trade wars and political conflicts. As a result, many students are interested in understanding global communications and entrepreneurial studies to ensure that they are not left behind in old business culture and outdated technology.

The rise of EdTech (Education Technology) companies like Enterprise College has made it easier than ever for students to access high-quality education in global communications and entrepreneurial studies. These companies use innovative teaching methods, such as immersive experiential learning, to give students the knowledge and skills they need to succeed in the modern business world. By partnering with BPOs (Business Processing Outsourcing) and using a scalable on-demand workforce, these companies are able to offer cost-effective and widely available education to students around the world.

In addition to providing students with a global educational experience, EdTech companies like Enterprise College also prepare students for the modern job market. As businesses become increasingly globalized and technology-dependent, employers are looking for candidates with strong communication skills and a modern entrepreneurial mindset. By teaching students how to communicate effectively across cultures and think creatively in the face of complex challenges, EdTech companies are helping students develop the skills they need to succeed in the 21st century workplace.

Furthermore, students who study global communications and entrepreneurial studies are also more likely to become leaders in their communities and make a positive impact on the world. By understanding how to communicate effectively and think critically about complex global issues, students can become agents of change in their communities and work towards creating a more just and equitable world.

The benefits of studying global communications and entrepreneurial studies are not just limited to the business world. Students who have a deep understanding of these topics are also better equipped to navigate the complexities of modern life. Whether it's communicating with family and friends from different cultural backgrounds or understanding the impact of global issues on their daily lives, students who have studied these topics have a broader perspective on the world around them.

Moreover, the rise of remote virtual online learning has made it easier than ever for students to access global communications and entrepreneurial studies courses from anywhere in the world. With a reliable internet connection, students can participate in virtual classrooms and connect with students and educators from all over the world. This has made it easier for students to gain a global perspective on the issues that matter most to them and to learn from the best educators in the field.

students today are increasingly aware of the importance of global communications and entrepreneurial studies. By studying these topics, students can gain a deeper understanding of the world around them and develop the skills they need to succeed in the modern business world. EdTech companies like Enterprise College are at the forefront of this movement, offering innovative and cost-effective education to students around the world. With the rise of remote virtual online learning, the opportunities for students to study these topics are greater than ever before, giving young learners the chance to gain a global perspective and make a positive impact on the world.

TEACHERS TOMORROW

As technology continues to advance and the next generation of students becomes more tech-savvy, the need for modern educational methodologies and technology in the classroom is greater than ever before. However, many teachers have fallen behind in these areas, leaving students feeling disconnected and unengaged in traditional learning environments.

In today's fast-paced and ever-evolving world, students are looking for more engaging and experiential learning experiences. They want to learn in a way that feels relevant and applicable to their lives, and they want to use technology to help them do so. This is where Enterprise College comes in, as it offers a modern, immersive, and experiential learning environment that is tailored to the needs of the modern student.

The Enterprise College model is designed to provide students with an engaging and interactive learning experience that combines technology and experiential learning methodologies. By immersing students in real-world scenarios and providing them with hands-on experience, Enterprise College is able to bridge the gap between traditional education and the modern world.

However, for this model to be truly effective, teachers must also adapt to this style of education. They must be willing to learn and incorporate new technologies and methodologies into their teaching strategies. This means embracing new tools and technologies, such as virtual and augmented reality, and incorporating them into the classroom.

Furthermore, teachers must also be willing to take a more consultative approach to teaching, which involves working closely with students to understand their unique learning needs and tailoring their teaching strategies accordingly. This requires a deep understanding of the individual needs of each student and a willingness to adapt teaching styles to fit those needs.

Additionally, teachers must be able to work effectively with technology, which can be a challenge for those who are not comfortable with technology or who are not familiar with the latest trends and tools. This requires ongoing training and education, as well as a willingness to experiment and try new things.

Enterprise College offers a unique opportunity for teachers to learn and grow in this way, as it provides a supportive and immersive learning environment that is focused on helping teachers and students stay up-to-date with the latest trends and technologies. By working closely with other educators and technology experts, teachers can develop new skills and strategies that will help them better serve their students.

Moreover, Enterprise College also provides a unique opportunity for teachers to work with students from around the world, which can be a valuable learning experience in and of itself. By engaging with students from different cultures and backgrounds, teachers can gain a deeper understanding of the world and develop new perspectives on teaching and learning.

So for now, Enterprise College is a model for modern immersive experiential learning that is tailored to the needs of the modern student. However, for this model to be truly effective, teachers must also adapt to this style of education and be willing to embrace new technologies and methodologies. By doing so, they can provide their students with the engaging and relevant educational experience that they need to thrive in the modern world.

THE FUTURE

Professional and career development through global communications studies has become increasingly important for future generations of students. With the world becoming more interconnected, businesses are seeking employees with a global perspective and the ability to communicate effectively across cultural and geographic boundaries.

As the pace of globalization continues to accelerate, students are looking for a global educational experience that will help them learn professional business and entrepreneurial ways to communicate in an ever-faster moving and evolving world. Students recognize that in order to succeed in today's global marketplace, they need to be able to communicate with people from diverse backgrounds and cultures.

Global communication studies offer students the opportunity to develop skills in cross-cultural communication, intercultural competence, and global leadership. These skills are becoming increasingly important as more and more businesses are expanding globally and seeking employees who can effectively navigate and communicate in diverse cultural settings.

Furthermore, global communication studies also provide students with a deep understanding of the role of communication in shaping global events, from international politics to global business. This understanding is essential for students who aspire to work in fields such as international relations, diplomacy, or global business.

Studying global communication also exposes students to a range of professional and career opportunities, from working as a journalist or public relations specialist to working in international development or corporate communications. The ability to communicate effectively across cultures and borders is a highly valued skill in these fields and can lead to exciting and rewarding careers.

In addition, global communication studies can also help students to develop critical thinking skills and become more aware of global issues and challenges. This awareness is important for students who want to make a positive impact on the world and contribute to global solutions.

Moreover, with the growth of technology and the internet, global communication has become more important than ever. The ability to communicate effectively across cultures and languages is essential for businesses to operate and compete in the global marketplace. As such, students who are proficient in global communication skills are in high demand by employers.

Finally, global communication studies provide students with an opportunity to learn about diverse cultures and perspectives, which is critical for fostering empathy and understanding in today's interconnected world. By developing a deep understanding of different cultures, students can become global citizens who are equipped to tackle complex global challenges and contribute to a more peaceful and prosperous world.

Overall, professional and career development through global communication studies is crucial for future generations of students. It offers students the opportunity to develop critical skills, gain a deep understanding of global issues, and become global citizens who are equipped to tackle complex global challenges.

GLOBAL COMMUNITY

The global community is a diverse and complex network of nations and cultures that span the globe. Each region, including Asia, the Middle East, Europe, Russia, Latin America, the United States, the UK, and Australia, has its own unique history, culture, and economic and political systems that shape its relationship with the rest of the world.

Asia is the world's largest continent, home to more than half of the world's population. It is a diverse region with many distinct cultures, languages, and religions. It is also home to some of the world's fastest-growing economies, such as China and India, and has become a hub for global trade and innovation.

The Middle East is a region that has been at the center of global geopolitics for centuries. It is home to some of the world's oldest civilizations, including those of Egypt, Mesopotamia, and Persia. It is also the birthplace of Islam, Christianity, and Judaism, which have shaped the region's culture and politics.

Europe is a continent with a rich history and culture that has influenced the world in countless ways. It is home to some of the world's oldest and most prominent universities, as well as some of the world's largest economies. It has also been the site of many wars and conflicts, which have shaped its political and social systems.

Russia is the world's largest country, spanning two continents and multiple time zones. It has a rich cultural heritage, with a history that spans more than a millennium. It is also a major player in global geopolitics, with significant influence over the political and economic systems of neighboring countries.

Latin America is a diverse region that spans from Mexico to the southern tip of South America. It is home to a variety of cultures and languages, and has a rich history that includes some of the world's oldest and most advanced civilizations. It is also the site of ongoing political and economic challenges, as many countries struggle to balance economic development with social and environmental concerns.

The United States is a global superpower, with the world's largest economy and military. It has a rich cultural heritage, with influences from all over the world. It is also a leader in innovation and technology, and has been at the forefront of many important global initiatives.

The UK is a small island nation with a rich cultural heritage that has influenced the world in many ways. It is a leader in many industries, including finance, education, and technology. It has also played an important role in global politics, particularly in the European Union.

Australia is a unique continent and country, with a diverse landscape and culture that has been shaped by its isolation from the rest of the world. It is home to some of the world's oldest indigenous cultures, as well as a vibrant and diverse modern society. It is also a leader in many areas, including renewable energy and environmental protection.

Despite these differences, the global community is connected in many ways. Advances in technology, transportation, and communication have made it easier than ever for people from different regions to interact and collaborate. Global challenges such as climate change, economic inequality, and political instability require cooperation and coordination among nations and cultures.

As the world becomes increasingly interconnected, it is important for individuals and institutions to understand the differences and similarities among different regions of the global community. By working together and respecting each other's differences, we can create a more just, peaceful, and prosperous world for all.

EDTECH&ONLINE

The traditional college education experience has been transformed by the evolution of EdTech (Education Technology) over the last decade. Students now have more choices and greater opportunities to learn and explore new international experiences without being limited by cost and distance.

One of the biggest benefits of EdTech is the flexibility it offers students. Rather than being confined to a traditional classroom, students can now learn from anywhere in the world, at any time that is convenient for them. This is particularly beneficial for students who may have work or family obligations that make attending traditional classes difficult.

In addition, EdTech provides students with access to a wider range of courses and programs. Rather than being limited by what is offered at their local college or university, students can now choose from a range of online programs and courses from top universities around the world.

EdTech also provides students with greater opportunities for personalized learning. Online platforms can track a student's progress and provide customized feedback and support based on their individual needs and learning style. This can lead to better academic outcomes and increased student engagement.

Furthermore, EdTech provides students with opportunities to learn new skills and gain expertise in emerging fields. For example, students can now access online courses in data science, artificial intelligence, and cybersecurity, which are in high demand in today's job market.

Another benefit of EdTech is its ability to create a more inclusive learning environment. Students from all backgrounds and walks of life can now access quality education, regardless of their socioeconomic status, geographic location, or physical ability.

In addition, EdTech provides opportunities for international collaboration and cultural exchange. Students can now connect with peers from around the world, share ideas, and learn about different cultures and perspectives. This can lead to increased cultural understanding and empathy.

EdTech also offers cost savings for students. Online courses and programs are often more affordable than traditional college courses, and students can save on expenses such as housing and transportation.

Furthermore, EdTech can help reduce the carbon footprint of education. By eliminating the need for students to travel to and from classes, online learning can reduce greenhouse gas emissions and contribute to a more sustainable future.

However, it is important to note that EdTech is not a replacement for traditional college education. While online learning can provide flexibility and accessibility, it is important to have a well-rounded education that includes in-person interactions and hands-on experiences.

Overall, the evolution of EdTech has transformed the traditional college education experience, offering students greater choice, flexibility, and access to a wider range of courses and programs. As technology continues to evolve, the possibilities for education are endless, and students can look forward to an exciting and dynamic learning experience.

ONLINE LEARNING

As technology continues to evolve at a rapid pace, future generations of young learners are desiring a global educational experience that is both immersive and accessible. Remote virtual online learning has emerged as a popular option for students who are seeking to expand their educational opportunities beyond the traditional classroom setting.

One of the key benefits of remote virtual online learning is that it allows students to access education from anywhere in the world. This means that students can study with experts and professionals from around the globe, giving them a truly global perspective on their chosen field. By gaining exposure to different cultures and viewpoints, students are better prepared to succeed in the global marketplace.

Another benefit of remote virtual online learning is that it provides students with access to emerging fields of professional careers that require expertise in global communications, entrepreneurial studies, intentional business, strategic technology, and more. These fields are rapidly evolving and require a deep understanding of the latest trends and practices. By studying online, students can gain access to the latest insights and expertise from industry leaders around the world.

In addition, remote virtual online learning is often more flexible than traditional classroom learning. This allows students to study at their own pace and on their own schedule, which can be especially beneficial for those who are working or have other commitments. This flexibility also allows students to customize their learning experience to suit their individual needs and learning style.

Remote virtual online learning also provides students with the opportunity to develop important skills such as self-discipline, time management, and digital literacy. These skills are increasingly important in today's rapidly changing world and can help students to succeed both academically and professionally.

Another advantage of remote virtual online learning is that it often uses modern and evolving technology, such as video conferencing, virtual reality, and artificial intelligence. These technologies can enhance the learning experience and provide students with new and innovative ways to engage with the material. By using these technologies, students can gain a deeper understanding of complex concepts and develop the skills they need to succeed in their chosen field.

Finally, remote virtual online learning is often more cost-effective than traditional classroom learning. This can make education more accessible to students who may not have the financial resources to attend a traditional college or university. By providing affordable education, remote virtual online learning can help to democratize access to education and create more opportunities for students around the world.

In summary, future generations of young learners are seeking a global educational experience that is immersive, accessible, and flexible. Remote virtual online learning provides a solution that allows students to access emerging fields of professional careers, develop important skills, use modern and evolving technology, and do so in a cost-effective manner. As technology continues to evolve and the demand for global education grows, remote virtual online learning is poised to become an increasingly popular and effective option for students around the world.

EDTECH WORKFORCE

In the future, colleges will need to adapt to the changing landscape of higher education by leveraging an on-demand, scalable workforce to reduce operational costs and maximize teaching talent acquisition. This approach will allow colleges to remain competitive, attract top talent, and offer innovative programs that meet the evolving needs of students.

The on-demand workforce model will enable colleges to hire teachers and support staff as needed, without the burden of traditional employment contracts. This will allow institutions to be more agile and responsive to changes in demand, while reducing fixed labor costs.

The on-demand model will also help colleges to tap into a wider pool of talent. Institutions will be able to hire teachers and support staff from around the world, rather than being limited to a local talent pool. This will enable colleges to recruit the best and brightest, regardless of location.

In addition, online teaching and learning will continue to grow in popularity as students seek greater global opportunities that only EdTech institutions can offer. Colleges will need to embrace this trend and invest in modern online technology to deliver high-quality programs to students around the world.

Online learning has many advantages over traditional face-to-face learning. It allows students to learn at their own pace, on their own schedule, and from anywhere in the world. This flexibility is especially important for working adults who need to balance their education with their professional and personal lives.

Online learning also offers students a greater variety of courses and programs. Colleges can offer courses that may not be feasible in a traditional classroom setting due to cost or logistical constraints. This means that students can access a wider range of educational opportunities and customize their learning experience to suit their individual needs and interests.

Moreover, online learning is often more affordable than traditional face-to-face learning. By leveraging technology, colleges can reduce the cost of delivering educational content, which translates into lower tuition fees for students.

Online learning also fosters collaboration and community-building. Through online discussion forums and virtual classrooms, students can connect with their peers and teachers from around the world. This global perspective can enrich the learning experience and prepare students for success in a globalized economy.

However, face-to-face learning still has its proper place in higher education. It provides students with valuable opportunities for hands-on learning, such as laboratory experiments, clinical rotations, and fieldwork. It also allows students to build relationships with their teachers and peers in a more personal way.

Colleges of the future will need to strike a balance between online and face-to-face learning to provide students with the best of both worlds. This hybrid approach will enable institutions to offer a more personalized and flexible educational experience that meets the diverse needs of students.

To achieve this balance, colleges will need to invest in modern technology that supports both online and face-to-face learning. This may include video conferencing software, learning management systems, and virtual reality tools.

In addition, colleges will need to develop new pedagogical approaches that are suited to online and hybrid learning. This may involve designing courses that are more interactive, collaborative, and experiential, and incorporating new technologies such as gamification and adaptive learning.

Finally, colleges will need to embrace a culture of innovation and continuous improvement. They will need to be open to experimentation and willing to take risks to stay ahead of the curve. By doing so, they can ensure that they remain relevant and competitive in a rapidly changing higher education landscape.

The colleges of the future must embrace an on-demand, scalable workforce to reduce operational costs and maximize talent acquisition while simultaneously investing in modern online technology to offer high-quality educational programs to students around the world. This hybrid approach that balances online and face-to-face learning will provide students with a personalized and flexible educational experience that meets their diverse needs. The colleges of the future must also develop new pedagogical approaches that leverage the latest technologies to provide interactive, collaborative, and experiential learning opportunities to students. Lastly, colleges must cultivate a culture of innovation and continuous improvement to stay ahead of the curve and remain relevant and competitive in the rapidly changing higher education landscape. By embracing these strategies, the colleges of the future can prepare students for success in a globalized economy and provide them with the tools they need to thrive in an increasingly interconnected world.

GEOPOLITICS & GEOECONOMICS

EdTech (Education Technology) and virtual online remote learning play a significant role in geopolitics and geoeconomics facing young learners today. The emergence of technology has revolutionized the education sector, allowing students to access education from anywhere in the world, breaking down geographic and cultural barriers.

One of the biggest geopolitical issues that students face is inequality in education access. Virtual online remote learning can help level the playing field by providing access to quality education for students who may not have had the opportunity otherwise. This can be particularly impactful in developing countries or areas with limited educational resources.

Another issue that students face is safety concerns, particularly in areas with political instability or conflict. Virtual online remote learning can provide a safe and secure learning environment for students, allowing them to continue their education without fear of violence or persecution.

In terms of geoeconomics, technology can help increase economic opportunities for students. For example, remote virtual online learning can provide access to specialized education and training that can lead to high-paying jobs in emerging fields, such as artificial intelligence, data science, and cybersecurity. This can help individuals and communities increase their economic well-being and reduce inequality.

Technology can also help students develop important cross-cultural communication and collaboration skills, which are becoming increasingly important in a globalized world. Through virtual online remote learning, students can interact with peers from different countries and backgrounds, expanding their worldview and fostering cultural understanding and empathy.

However, it is important to note that technology is not a panacea for all educational issues. It is crucial to ensure that virtual online remote learning platforms are safe and secure for students, with appropriate measures in place to protect privacy and prevent cyber threats.

In addition, technology should be used in conjunction with effective teaching methods and pedagogical strategies to ensure that students are learning effectively and efficiently. It is important to strike a balance between technology and traditional teaching methods to create a well-rounded educational experience for students.

Furthermore, it is important to consider the digital divide that still exists in many parts of the world. Access to technology and reliable internet is not universal, which can create further inequalities in education. Efforts must be made to bridge this digital divide and ensure that all students have equal access to educational opportunities.

Overall, EdTech and virtual online remote learning have the potential to play a significant role in shaping the geopolitics and geoeconomics facing young learners today. By providing access to quality education, creating safe and secure learning environments, increasing economic opportunities, and fostering cross-cultural communication and collaboration, technology can help create a brighter future for students around the world. However, it is important to approach technology with caution and ensure that it is used in an effective and responsible manner.

EDTECH STAFFING

The traditional model of staffing in higher education institutions can be a costly affair. Salaries, benefits, and overhead expenses can add up, ultimately driving up the cost of tuition. However, EdTech colleges, such as Enterprise College, have found a way to reduce these costs through a scalable crowdsourced on demand staffing methodology.

By leveraging a scalable on demand workforce, EdTech institutions can avoid the costs of hiring full-time staff and instead rely on a pool of talented and qualified professionals who can be activated when needed. This not only reduces overhead expenses but also allows for a more flexible and agile approach to staffing.

Furthermore, by tapping into a global workforce, EdTech institutions can benefit from a wider pool of talent and expertise, giving students access to instructors and staff who are leaders in their respective fields.

The use of modern technologies, such as the internet and connectivity, has also allowed EdTech institutions to expand their reach and offer greater opportunities to students. By partnering with other institutions and organizations, EdTech colleges can offer courses and programs that are more widely available and cost-effective.

Additionally, EdTech institutions can use data analytics and AI to better understand the needs and preferences of their students, allowing for more personalized and targeted educational experiences. This not only enhances the student experience but also helps to increase student retention rates.

Crowdsourcing staffing also enables institutions to tap into diverse perspectives and experiences, resulting in a more inclusive learning environment. Students are exposed to a wider range of ideas and perspectives, ultimately leading to a more enriching educational experience.

Furthermore, the use of a scalable on demand staffing methodology can also help to reduce the administrative burden on faculty and staff, freeing up their time to focus on student engagement and success. This can ultimately lead to better academic outcomes and increased student satisfaction.

In addition, the scalability of the staffing methodology also allows EdTech institutions to adjust their staffing needs based on demand. This means that institutions can quickly and efficiently respond to changes in enrollment and course demand, ensuring that resources are allocated where they are needed most.

Ultimately, the use of a scalable on demand staffing methodology in EdTech institutions can help to reduce tuition costs and increase access to quality education. With the continued evolution of technology and connectivity, EdTech colleges can continue to expand their reach and offer students greater opportunities for success.

BEING DIFFERENT

In today's digital age, EdTech companies have emerged as disruptors in the traditional education sector. EdTech refers to companies that develop and provide educational technology products and services, which can range from online learning platforms and digital textbooks to personalized learning tools and educational games. These companies leverage technology to provide new and innovative ways to teach and learn, and are increasingly popular among students, educators, and institutions alike.

Enterprise College is a specialized online virtual college that partners with BPOs (Business Processing Outsourcing) to provide a unique approach to education. By leveraging a scalable on-demand workforce in four key areas of technology, operations, client relations, and audit, Enterprise College is able to operate internationally in different time zones around the world. This enables students to access education from anywhere in the world, at any time, and in a format that suits their learning needs.

One of the key advantages of Enterprise College is its ability to offer accreditation for its programs. This means that students who complete a program at Enterprise College can receive academic credit that is recognized by institutions around the world. This accreditation allows students to use their learning at Enterprise College to further their academic or professional pursuits, and demonstrates the value of the education they have received.

Another advantage of Enterprise College is its focus on experiential learning. This means that students are not just learning theoretical concepts, but are also gaining practical experience in their chosen field. By providing students with hands-on experience, Enterprise College enables students to gain real-world skills that are directly applicable to their future careers. This focus on experiential learning sets Enterprise College apart from other EdTech companies and provides a unique value proposition for students.

Enterprise College is also highly specialized in four areas of technology, operations, client relations, and audit. This specialization enables the college to provide high-quality education in these areas, and ensures that students receive a comprehensive understanding of the subject matter. By focusing on these areas, Enterprise College is able to provide a more targeted and effective education that is directly applicable to the needs of the industry.

In addition, Enterprise College's partnership with BPOs enables the college to provide a unique approach to education. By working with BPOs, Enterprise College is able to provide students with access to a global network of industry experts and professionals. This enables students to learn from the best in their field and gain insights into the latest industry trends and practices.

Finally, Enterprise College's scalable on-demand workforce is a key advantage in the rapidly evolving field of EdTech. As demand for online education continues to grow, Enterprise College is able to quickly and easily scale its workforce to meet this demand. This scalability ensures that the college can provide a high-quality education to students around the world, while also enabling it to adapt to changes in the industry and the needs of its students.

In summary, Enterprise College is a specialized online virtual college that provides a unique approach to education. By partnering with BPOs, offering accreditation, focusing on experiential learning, and specializing in four key areas, Enterprise College sets itself apart from other EdTech companies. Its scalable on-demand workforce and global reach also position it for success in the rapidly evolving field of EdTech.

ENTERPRISE COLLEGE

Welcome to Enterprise College, where we take pride in providing top-notch education for professional and career development. Our focus on global communications studies has earned us a reputation as a leader in the industry. We are fully accredited by renowned agencies, including BPO, ensuring that our students receive the highest quality education. Our commitment to reaching international students and global corporate clients is unwavering, making us the perfect choice for those seeking a truly global education.

At Enterprise College, we are committed to providing our students with the best possible education, no matter where they are in the world. It's the hub of excellence in entrepreneurial studies and global communications. Our consortium comprises award-winning subsidiaries, recognized educational affiliates, and international partners who collaborate to provide you with the best academic experience.

We take pride in working with global partner BPOs and international agencies across Asia, Middle East, Europe, Russia, the UK, United States, and South America. As a result, we are fully accredited by partnering with international agencies and educational institutions.

At Enterprise College, we have a unique approach to staffing. We use a crowdsourced scalable on-demand workforce using the TOCA framework, which allows for international access via BPOs globally. This enables us to offer F2F Workshop Seminars and online Masterclass Webinars that are released globally.

Our commitment to excellence is reflected in our accreditations, including TESOL & TEYL certifications to support international students and guests focusing on global communication studies.

Welcome to Enterprise College, where education meets inspiration! Our college is proud to be the birthplace of the renowned Professor Lecture Series, which ran from 2004 to 2015. Over the course of those eleven years, we hosted 18 captivating lectures on various topics across 52 venues in seven states throughout New York and New England.

But that's not all! In 2017, we launched our exciting Professor Lecture Tour, which continues to this day. Our latest tour is focused on entrepreneurship and features a fantastic workshop seminar called "Publish Your Book Guaranteed." This event is a must-attend for anyone looking to turn their ideas into a published work.

At Enterprise College, we are dedicated to providing our students with the best possible education. That's why we offer a wealth of online resources, including courses, books, and videos, that can be accessed from anywhere, at any time. So why wait? Join us today and unlock your full potential!

Welcome to Enterprise College - where the world of entrepreneurship and global communications come together to create a unique educational experience for students around the globe. Our consortium is made up of award-winning subsidiaries, innovative incubators, and internationally recognized educational affiliates, all collaborating to provide the best academic programs in business, education, and science/technology.

At Enterprise College, we believe in the power of partnerships. That's why we work closely with global partner BPOs and international agencies across Asia, the Middle East, Europe, Russia, the UK, United States and South America to bring our students the best possible education. Our commitment to excellence has earned us full accreditation from partnering international agencies and educational institutions.

Our staff is made up of a crowdsourced scalable on-demand workforce, using the TOCA framework to provide international access via BPOs globally. Our presentations and services are available in a variety of formats, from face-to-face workshop seminars to online masterclass webinars, which are released globally.

We are also home to a number of exciting initiatives, including the Professor Lecture Series (2004-2015), which covered 18 topics at 52 venues across seven states in New York and New England which includes the Entrepreneur Workshop Seminar: Publish Your Book Guaranteed.

We pride ourselves on being a cutting-edge company that operates with a dynamic and scalable on-demand workforce. We have a team of 95 individuals who are experts in the Tech, Operations, Client, and Audit (TOCA) framework. Our accreditation comes from our trusted partners in Business Process Outsourcing (BPO) who provide us with the best talent in the industry.

Our team is composed of remote freelance agents who are assigned to specific tasks under the TOCA framework. Each member is allocated tasks that can range from 5 minutes to several hours, depending on the complexity of the assignment. Our TOCA framework is designed to ensure that all tasks are completed efficiently and effectively.

We work with BPOs that are established in different countries around the world, allowing us to reach a global audience. Our team is managed by Enterprise College, and we use the TOCA framework to ensure that all tasks are completed to the highest standard.

The TOCA framework stands for Technology, Operations, Client Relations, and Audit. Our BPO partners provide us with the best talent in these areas, ensuring that we can deliver our services to clients across Asia, the Middle East, Europe, Russia, and Latin America.

At Enterprise College, we understand the importance of using the latest technology to ensure that our team can work remotely. We use VPN, portals, and firewalls to ensure that our team can connect to our clients' networks securely. Our operations team ensures that we can schedule tasks across different time zones, while our client relations team focuses on marketing and sales. Finally, our audit team takes care of finance processing, AR, and AP.

In summary, we are a dynamic and innovative company that operates with a scalable on-demand workforce. We work with BPOs to provide the best talent in the industry and use the TOCA framework to ensure that all tasks are completed to the highest standard. Our global reach allows us to deliver our services to clients around the world, and our use of the latest technology ensures that we can work remotely and securely.

FOUNDER&CEO

Meet Ambassador Professor, Dr. David K. Ewen, a sought-after educator and entrepreneur with a global reputation since 1988. This award-winning professor has been making waves in the education industry, sharing his expertise in global communication and entrepreneurial studies across business, education, and digital multimedia technology.

With years of experience teaching English around the world, Dr. Ewen has become a respected authority in the field, working with EdTech companies since 2014. He's also an accomplished author, speaker, and podcaster, sharing his insights and knowledge with students and professionals alike.

Dr. Ewen's impressive academic credentials include a Master of Education earned in 1988 and a Doctor of Education degree he's currently pursuing, set for completion in 2023. His thesis, titled "Achieving M.O.D.E.L.S. of Excellence," is already making waves and is filed with Open Education Resource Commons.

If you're looking for Dr. Ewen's work, you can find his many books and audiobook performances at Enterprise College. In the private sector, he specializes in business, education, and technology, bringing his unique perspective and expertise to help businesses and organizations thrive.

But that's not all. Dr. Ewen's successful Professor Lecture Tour from 2004 to 2015 was a hit among students and professionals, specializing in digital multimedia technology, global communications, and entrepreneurial studies. His presentations are LIVE workshop seminars on stage and online masterclass webinars, always engaging, informative, and inspiring.

METHODOLOGY

The style of education that comes from Enterprise College is quite unique, as it emphasizes a consultative immersion approach. In this approach, students and clients are not merely taught theory but rather they are fully immersed in the life of what they are trying to learn. This style of education emphasizes experiential learning, where students are encouraged to learn by doing. Rather than being passive recipients of information, they are active participants in their own learning process.

At Enterprise College, the consultative immersion style of education is designed to be highly personalized. Each student and client has a unique set of goals and aspirations, and the college works closely with them to develop a customized learning experience that meets their needs. This approach enables students and clients to learn in a way that suits their learning style, preferences, and interests. They are also able to receive ongoing feedback and guidance from their instructors, which helps them to stay on track and make progress towards their goals.

One of the key benefits of the consultative immersion style of education is that it is highly practical. By living the life of what they are trying to learn, students and clients are able to apply the skills and knowledge they acquire in real-world situations. This approach helps to build confidence and competence, and it also enables students and clients to develop a deeper understanding of the subject matter. They are also able to see the direct impact of their learning on their own lives and the lives of those around them.

Another advantage of the consultative immersion style of education is that it fosters collaboration and teamwork. By working together to solve problems and achieve goals, students and clients are able to develop strong relationships and learn from each other. This approach also helps to build a sense of community and shared purpose, which can be highly motivating and inspiring. Students and clients are encouraged to support each other and celebrate their successes, which creates a positive and supportive learning environment.

In conclusion, the consultative immersion style of education offered by Enterprise College is a highly effective approach that emphasizes practical learning, personalized instruction, and collaborative teamwork. By living the life of what they are trying to learn, students and clients are able to develop the skills, knowledge, and experience they need to succeed in the real world. This approach fosters a strong sense of community and shared purpose, which makes learning a rewarding and enjoyable experience.

EXPERIENTIAL IMMERSISIVE LEARNING

Experiential and immersive learning online is an approach to education that focuses on hands-on learning experiences that are designed to simulate real-world scenarios. This type of learning is particularly effective in fields like global communications and entrepreneurial studies where students need to be able to apply their skills and knowledge in practical settings. The key to success with experiential and immersive learning online is motivation, organization, discipline, ethics, lifelong learning, and discipline for studying.

Motivation is critical when it comes to experiential and immersive learning online. Students who are motivated to learn will be more engaged and invested in the learning process. Motivation can come from a variety of sources, such as a passion for the subject matter, a desire to learn new skills, or a sense of purpose. One way to boost motivation is to create a learning environment that is fun and interactive. For example, online simulations and games can be used to make learning more engaging and exciting.

Organization is also important when it comes to experiential and immersive learning online. Students need to be able to manage their time effectively and stay on top of their coursework. This requires strong organizational skills, such as setting goals, creating schedules, and prioritizing tasks. One way to improve organization is to use online tools and resources, such as calendars, task lists, and reminders.

Discipline is another key factor in successful experiential and immersive learning online.

Students need to be able to stay focused and motivated even when the learning process becomes challenging or tedious. This requires self-discipline, which can be fostered through regular practice and reinforcement. One way to build discipline is to set regular study times and stick to them, even when other distractions arise.

Ethics are an important consideration in experiential and immersive learning online, particularly in fields like global communications and entrepreneurial studies where students may encounter ethical dilemmas. Students need to be able to identify ethical issues and make sound decisions that are consistent with their values and beliefs. This requires critical thinking skills and a strong sense of ethics. One way to build ethical awareness is to engage in discussions and debates about ethical issues and to explore case studies that illustrate different ethical perspectives.

Lifelong learning is a key component of experiential and immersive learning online. Students need to be able to adapt to new technologies and changing industry trends in order to stay competitive in the job market. This requires a commitment to ongoing learning and professional development. One way to foster lifelong learning is to participate in online forums and communities where students can share ideas, network, and learn from each other.

Discipline for studying is also critical in experiential and immersive learning online. Students need to be able to manage their time effectively and stay on track with their coursework. This requires discipline and a strong work ethic. One way to build discipline for studying is to set clear goals and deadlines, and to break large assignments into smaller, manageable tasks.

In global communications and entrepreneurial studies, experiential and immersive learning online can take many forms. For example, students may participate in virtual simulations that allow them to practice communication and negotiation skills in a global business context. They may also engage in case studies and role-playing exercises that simulate real-world entrepreneurial scenarios. These types of experiences provide students with hands-on learning opportunities that help them develop practical skills that they can apply in their careers.

Online learning environments can also facilitate experiential and immersive learning by providing access to a variety of tools and resources. For example, students may use virtual reality technology to explore global business environments or to simulate the launch of a new product. They may also use online collaboration tools to work on group projects or to communicate with classmates and instructors.

One of the benefits of experiential and immersive learning online is that it can be tailored to the individual needs and preferences of students. For example, students who prefer a more visual or auditory learning experience can take advantage of online videos and interactive multimedia tools. Those who prefer a more hands-on approach can engage in virtual labs and simulations that allow them to practice skills in a safe and controlled environment.

In order to be successful with experiential and immersive learning online, students must also have access to high-quality instruction and support. Instructors should provide clear guidance and feedback, as well as opportunities for students to reflect on their learning and receive constructive criticism. Online forums and communities can also provide a valuable source of support, allowing students to share ideas and collaborate with peers and instructors.

Another important factor to consider when implementing experiential and immersive learning online is the need for assessment and evaluation. It is important to have clear learning objectives and to use appropriate assessment tools to measure student progress and mastery. This can include formative assessments like quizzes and assignments, as well as summative assessments like final projects and exams.

Finally, it is important to recognize the potential challenges and limitations of experiential and immersive learning online. For example, online simulations and games may not always accurately reflect real-world scenarios, and students may face technical difficulties or limitations when using virtual reality or other immersive technologies. Instructors and students must be prepared to adapt and adjust as needed to ensure that the learning experience is effective and meaningful.

In conclusion, experiential and immersive learning online can be a highly effective approach to education in fields like global communications and entrepreneurial studies. By focusing on motivation, organization, discipline, ethics, lifelong learning, and discipline for studying, students can develop practical skills and knowledge that they can apply in their careers. With access to high-quality instruction and support, and a commitment to ongoing assessment and evaluation, experiential and immersive learning online can help students succeed in a rapidly changing and competitive job market.

CULTURE & DIVERSITY

Enterprise College is an educational institution that operates in different cultures around the world, including Asia, the Middle East, Europe, Russia, Latin America, the U.K., and the United States. The college has a strong commitment to cultural sensitivity and diversity, and this is reflected in the way it operates in each region.

In Asia, Enterprise College works closely with local partners to develop customized educational programs that meet the specific needs of students and clients. The college has a deep understanding of the cultural nuances in this region, and this enables it to deliver effective and impactful educational experiences.

In the Middle East, Enterprise College places a strong emphasis on respecting cultural traditions and values. The college works closely with local organizations and leaders to ensure that its educational programs are culturally sensitive and appropriate.

In Europe, Russia, and the U.K., Enterprise College operates in a highly diverse environment with a wide range of cultural backgrounds. The college has a strong focus on cross-cultural communication and sensitivity, and it works closely with students and clients to ensure that their needs are met in a culturally appropriate manner.

In Latin America, Enterprise College is committed to working with local communities and organizations to provide education and training that is relevant to the local context. The college has a deep understanding of the cultural diversity in this region, and this enables it to provide tailored educational experiences that meet the unique needs of its clients.

One of the biggest challenges of working online virtually with different cultures is the potential for miscommunication and misunderstandings. To be successful in this context, it is important to establish clear lines of communication and to be sensitive to cultural differences. This may involve using translation tools or hiring bilingual staff to ensure that everyone is on the same page.

Another challenge is the need to adapt to different time zones and working hours. Enterprise College works closely with its clients to establish a schedule that works for everyone, and it uses technology to facilitate remote communication and collaboration.

To be successful in working with different cultures online, it is also important to be aware of cultural norms and expectations. For example, in some cultures, it is considered impolite to disagree or say no outright, so it is important to be aware of these nuances and adjust communication accordingly.

Cultural sensitivity training is another key factor in successfully working with different cultures online. Enterprise College provides its staff and instructors with training on cultural awareness and sensitivity, which helps them to better understand and navigate the unique cultural contexts in which they operate.

Another important factor in working with different cultures online is the need to be flexible and adaptable. Different cultures may have different approaches to problem-solving, decision-making, and communication, and it is important to be open to new ideas and approaches.

Enterprise College also recognizes the importance of building relationships and trust in different cultural contexts. The college places a strong emphasis on building long-term relationships with its clients and partners, and it invests time and resources in cultivating these relationships over time.

In conclusion, Enterprise College operates in different cultural contexts around the world, and it is committed to cultural sensitivity and diversity. The college recognizes the challenges of working online virtually with different cultures, and it has developed strategies and approaches to address these challenges. By emphasizing clear communication, cultural sensitivity, and flexibility, Enterprise College is able to deliver effective and impactful educational experiences that meet the unique needs of its clients in different cultural contexts.

CONCLUSION

Thank you for taking the time to read about the EdTech model example of Enterprise College. We hope that our insights into experiential immersive online learning have been helpful in understanding the potential for this type of education. Our goal is to create a scalable and on-demand workforce from partner organizations, while also focusing on global communications and entrepreneurial studies.

At Enterprise College, we are dedicated to providing our students with the tools they need to succeed in the ever-changing world of business. Our focus on motivation, organization, discipline, ethics, lifelong learning, and the strength to not give up has helped to create students who are models of excellence. We believe that this is the key to success in any field, and we are committed to instilling these values in all of our students.

The world of education is constantly evolving, and we are excited to be at the forefront of this change. Our experiential immersive online learning model is designed to provide students with real-world experience and practical skills that they can apply to their future careers. We believe that this approach to education is the future, and we are committed to continuing to innovate and push the boundaries of what is possible in the field of EdTech.

Finally, we would like to express our gratitude to all of our students, partners, and supporters who have helped to make Enterprise College a success. Without your dedication and support, none of this would be possible. We are honored to be a part of the global community of educators who are working to shape the future of education, and we look forward to continuing to work with all of you to make a difference in the lives of our students and the world at large. Thank you again for reading, and we hope to see you soon at Enterprise College.

Dr. David K. Ewen

www.ingramcontent.com/pod-product-compliance
Lightning Source LLC
Chambersburg PA
CBHW070350220526
45467CB00001B/323